Love,

Zee

"*And when the Prayer is finished, then may ye disperse through the land, and seek the Bounty of Allah; and remember Allah frequently that ye may prosper.*"
(*Al Qur'an: Chapter 62, Verse 11*)

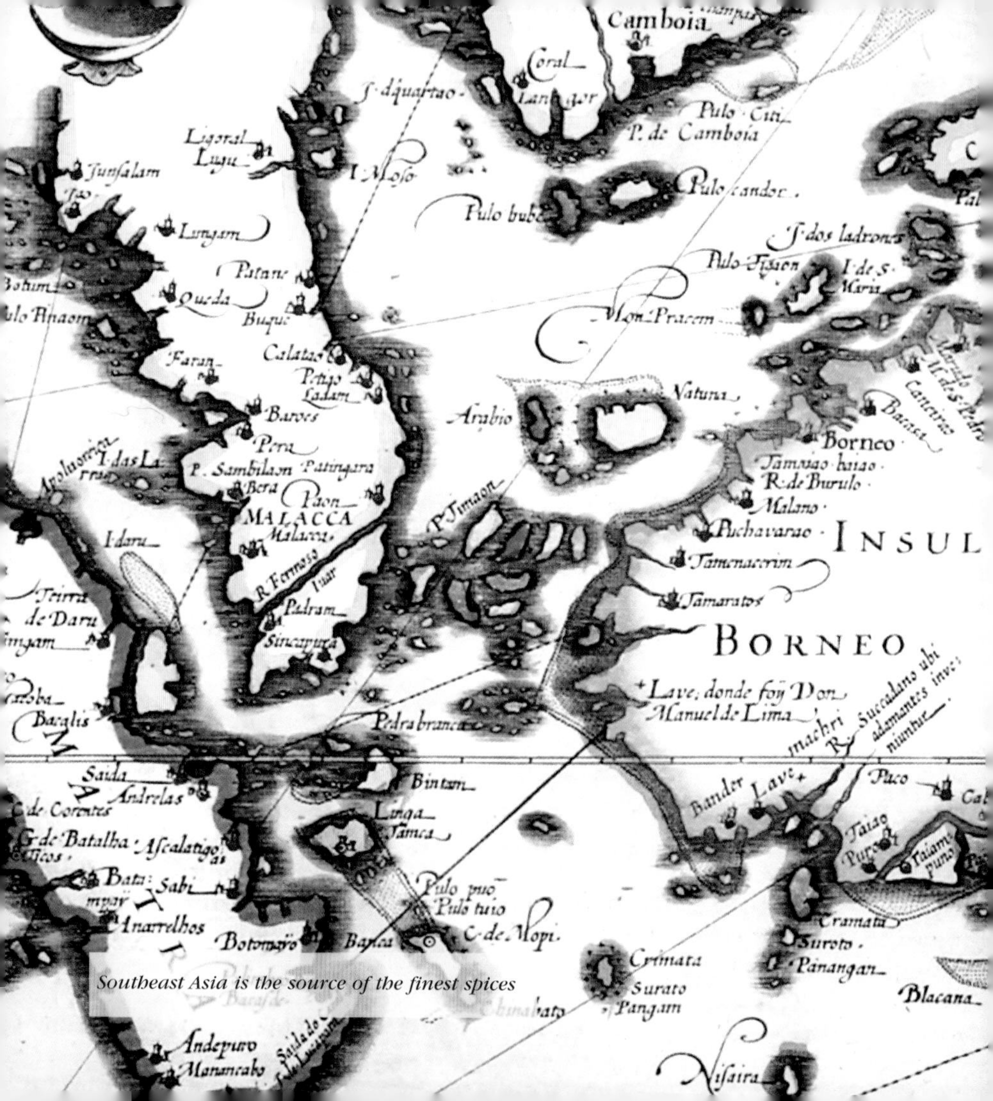

Southeast Asia is the source of the finest spices

LAGUS

S. LA ZARI.

Panama · Saburan · I. Caburao · J. Vean

Cabo · I. Abuyo

Negros · Pasage de S. Clara

Bofrote · Caragni · men

Cavangao · Mala qua · Surtea

Dapiw · B. de Malega · G. de Resurrei cam · I. de S. Jonnes

S. Michuel · Canola · MINDA NAO B · Mindanao · Bicaia · A. de Resurrie am

Praxel · Cangaxiri · Burun · C. de Bicay · I. de Palmeras

Sagina

Solor

Matao al: Cabins · Candinega · Caxango al: Sarangan

S. Joana · I. de Sagitti · I. de Talaon al: de Talavit

Baquenan

I. de Rao

Do Mou ro

MOLVCCÆ

Bangicae · Terrate · Gilolo la mar costa

Manado · I. de Dai

Pedory · Camafo

Tetolli de Celebre · Mutir · Maya

Duratis · Mich Tau

Saies · CE · Bachian · GILOLO INSULA

Momayo · INSULÆ · Cumit

Curicuri · Mandar

Tabuco · Ablato · Batachina · P. Canam

Cintuo

LE · Buorno · CEIR

Malist · Xulo al: os Papu

Supa · Tum · Xulla · I. Cenao · Ceibam

BES · Burro · Sinomo

Paqur · I. Cenaon

Jubon · Zelan · Palmes

Gugui

Pab

Publisher: Islamic Arts Museum Malaysia (IAMM)

Writers: Lucien de Guise and Zahir Sutarwala, Curatorial Department, IAMM

Design and photography: Aniza Ashaari, Alnurmarida Alias and Faizal Zahari,
Graphics and Photography Department, IAMM

Colour separation, printing and binding: MPH Group Printing (M) Sdn Bhd

© 2006 IAMM Publications
ISBN 983-40845-9-5

Perpustakaan Negara Malaysia   Cataloguing-in-Publication Data
Spice journeys : taste and trade in the Islamic world
ISBN 983-40845-9-5
1. Spice-History. 2. Spicy trade-History-Religious aspects-Islam
3. Trade routes-History. I. Muzium Kesenian Islam Malaysia.
641.338309

Contents

Introduction

Introduction

Islam and hospitality go together like coffee and cardamom. Islam and trade have also been inextricably bound since the time of the Prophet Muhammad ﷺ. As spices and aromatics provide unlimited opportunities for both activities, it is inevitable that the Islamic world has had a vital role to play. Important though this contribution is, it has rarely been publicised. The rampaging of conquistadores in Latin America or colonial conquest in Southeast Asia are what tend to fire the historical imagination. The activities of Muslim cultivators and merchants make for a quieter story. Tales from the *Thousand and One Nights* provide vivid splashes of colour, but otherwise there is little drama. In the same way that Islam spread gently through many lands, so did the trade in spices. The collection of the Islamic Arts Museum Malaysia is rich in artefacts that relate to this trade which shaped the modern world as well as innumerable lives over the centuries.

Chapter I

*"It is He Who has spread out the earth for (His) creatures.
Therein is fruit and date-palms, producing spathes. Also
corn, with leaves and stalk for fodder, and fragrant spices."*
(Al Qur'an Chapter 55, Verses 10-12)

The Spice of Countless Lives:
The importance of spices and aromatics

In Greek mythology, it was the face of Helen of Troy that launched a thousand ships. In reality, the quest for palatable food was the cause of far more maritime adventures. The Greeks were just one of many seafaring peoples in the early years of recorded history. Among the others were Phoenicians, Arabs and Indians. Their motivation was usually trade, rather than conquest, and the most tradable commodity was spices. Little has affected the history of the world as much as the sacks of small comestibles that have been transshipped for thousands of years.

Finding a satisfactory definition of spices is as difficult as it was to locate them originally. It is generally agreed that they must be organic, portable and highly valued for their taste or odour. Aromatics are included, even when not edible. Herbs are excluded as their worth is dependent on freshness, which was hardly a consideration at a time when a journey could take months. Some items that were considered spices in the past would not be admitted into the category nowadays. Sugar is a prominent example, as is coffee. Geography is another important factor; one man's prized spice is another's garden weed, depending on which part of the world they live in. One recurring feature of the most desirable spices is that they tended to be found in places that were not only inaccessible to Westerners but also to traders who were much closer to the source of the material. Chinese, Arab and Indian merchants were often as confused about the goods they sought as the Europeans who were prepared to pay so much for this exotica.

Where spices were involved, imaginations ran wild everywhere. The most entertaining – as well as the most informative – versions are in Arabic. Sinbad the Sailor was more of a spice trader than a sailor, and his adventures took him to places that people only went when in pursuit of huge profit. Cloves and cinnamon were two of Sinbad's most important cargoes around the 9th century. Seven hundred years later, lives were still being staked in the quest for Asia's most fabled wealth.

Spices lured the Portuguese to Asia and the Spanish to South America. The world of colonies was largely a result of this obsession. Earlier warriors were equally concerned. Alexander the Great was initially motivated by land hunger. He ended up with a passion for Eastern spices, considered unwholesome and un-Greek by many of his contemporaries. Before he reached Asia, Alexander had taken little interest in gastronomy, although as a boy he had been so wasteful with incense he was told to go out and conquer the lands in which they grew. The Muslim armies that swept through Asia and the Mediterranean world in the 7th century did not have spices or aromatics at the front of their minds. If they had, the Persians would not have mocked them for eating camphor under the illusion that it was salt. This might be a Persian myth, of course, as camphor was well known to the Arabs and is mentioned in no less an Arabic source than the Qur'an.

Long before history was recorded, mankind had been concerned about diet. Fire was useful for keeping away predators, but it was also found to improve the flavour of a meat source that might sustain people for weeks on end. Boredom with the same food also drove early man to create variety with seasonings. There would have been plenty of fatalities along the way, which must have been considered a price worth paying. Almonds are a classic case of a relatively deadly product that was developed at considerable risk to please the human palate. Early man also felt the need to appease supernatural tastes. Spices were used for

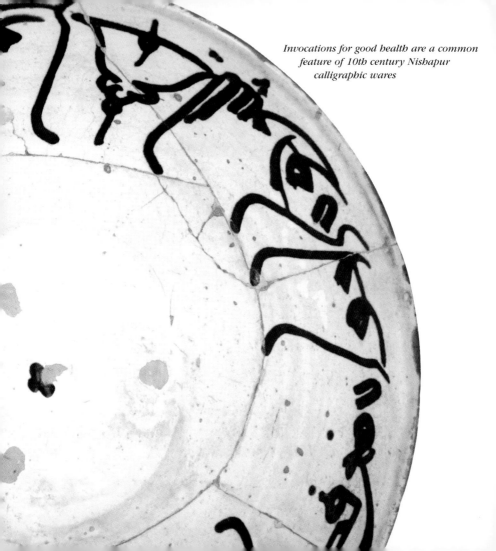

Invocations for good health are a common feature of 10th century Nishapur calligraphic wares

offerings to the gods in ancient Egypt and China. This later developed into banquets as expressions of power and divinity, furthering the association between good fare and food of the gods. The last supper of Jesus Christ might be seen as a continuation of this tradition.

Another vital function of spices was for health. This often included the preservation of the dead. In the case of Egyptian embalmers, essential spices comprised cinnamon, cassia and anise. The distinction between food and medicine was less pronounced in the past than it is now, unless one happens to be a traditionally minded modern Chinese gourmet, for whom the prophylactic value of any particular ingredient has to be taken into account.

In many ancient cultures, all three aspects of spices were valued. For the Egyptians it was cinnamon that started being cooked for pleasure several thousand years ago, while in China it was cassia. Originally from southern China, the Austronesian people who colonised the Pacific and Indian oceans would not have done without their ginger. This was probably the earliest spice to be part of international trade. Moving from island to island, among the most precious cargoes in their tiny outrigger boats was ginger root-stock to make life more bearable in their next home. Having settled in the Malay Peninsula and far to the west of that, their favourite spice later became essential to medicine in the Mediterranean world. Dioscorides the Greek physician considered it useful for a wide range of applications, including as a laxative and an antidote to poison. Back in its homeland of China, Confucius welcomed ginger into a diet that was as austere as his general philosophy of being.

As the most respected spices were those that were hardest to obtain, a network of trade routes needed to be established. This was a prototype of the globalised world in which we now live. The main difference is that in the past it would only have been the highest level of society that ever saw the bounty of far-off lands, while nowadays there are few people who do not own at least some moulded plastic from China.

Among the earliest spice traders were Arabs, who took over many routes as early as 900 BC. The importance of their merchandise was enormous. In the Middle East especially, demand was great enough for spices to be mentioned frequently in the Old Testament of the Bible. Joseph of the colourful coat was eventually bought by traders who were most probably transporting spices. When the Queen of Sheba visited King Solomon, it was south Arabian spices that were her most welcome gifts. The Greeks and Romans also took a keen interest in spices; unlike many ancient societies, they wrote about them extensively. The first dedicated cookery book is widely considered to be Apicius' *Art of Cooking,* written in the first century AD, or perhaps somewhat later. His recipes were no more aimed at the toiling masses than the gourmet fare of ancient Egypt, where meat was almost unknown to the pyramid-building proletariat. Fresh pepper on a pear souffle with fish sauce is one of his simpler signature dishes. Another of Apicius' favourite ingredients was asafoetida, a resinous spice that is now virtually unknown in Europe but is still popular in Arab and Indian cuisines.

Black pepper was an addiction for those Romans who could afford it. Serious gourmands went much further than that, although the myth of a thoroughly debauched empire owes more to fraternity toga-party fantasies than to Apicius. Other writers at the time often took a more disapproving view of the culinary arts. Pliny the Elder complained in the 1st century AD that 100 million *sestertii* a year was spent by Romans on spices and aromatics from India, China and the Arabian peninsula. It is easy to see how, when one examines the free-spending ways of a fictional character from *The Satyricon*. At the same time as Pliny, the writer Petronius introduced readers to Trimalchio, the crassest millionaire in Rome. Spices such as cumin and saffron do not just turn up in the food, they are also scattered on the floor as a simulation of sawdust.

Trimalchio is a parody of nouveau riche excess. His dishes were so bizarre, they went far beyond any effect that spices are capable of. The host has been called the first performance artist with food, although his fortune actually came from trading. He was a merchant, and it is made clear that this class could make enormous sums of money. His career was established on a combination of bacon, beans, slaves and spices.

The fall of the Roman empire did not bring about a democratisation of food. Exotic fare remained expensive, and merchants continued to prosper. Spices in medieval Europe were viewed in the same medicinal light as they were in Asia. Achieving a balance between 'hot' and 'cold' became a universal concern, and in almost every society the way to achieve this was with spices. In the Islamic world, people were not just traders in these commodities, they were also avid consumers. From the outset, Islam emphasised cleanliness and hygiene. Luxury was not encouraged, and certainly not the hedonism of ancient Rome or Persia. Still, a few pleasures of the flesh have always been permitted, within the official guidelines. People and food were allowed to look and smell good. This was an entirely alien approach to most European societies at the dawn of Islam.

Rosewater sprinklers are found throughout the Islamic world, including many from China

In Europe the main concern was health – keeping the 'four humours' in harmony. For Muslims there was a broader approach. In the hadith, it is recorded by Abu Said: "I testify that Allah's Apostle said, 'The taking of a bath on Friday is compulsory for every male Muslim who has attained the age of puberty and (also) the cleaning of his teeth with Siwak, and the using of perfume if it is available'." The Prophet's attachment to fragrances is well known, immortalised in numerous hadith. Less commonly attested to is his interest in food, although there are many references to spices as medicine: "There is healing in black cumin for all diseases except death." His views on spices for gastronomic pleasure are not recorded. However, the Qur'an assures those who reach paradise that in addition to a fountain of camphor, they "will be given to drink a cup tempered with ginger."

Ginger and camphor are the two extremes of 'hot' and 'cold', a concept that is explored thoroughly in *Medicine of the Prophet*, compiled by Ibn Qayyim al-Jawaziyya in the 14th century. The meat of cows was considered to be "cold, dry and hard to digest." Eating it in excess could bring on anything from leprosy to elephantiasis, unless "its harm has been removed with pepper, garlic, cinnamon, ginger and such like." Spices were clearly an essential part of early Islamic cuisine, and have remained so ever since. The great Sufi master Mevlana Jalaluddin Rumi used food as a metaphor in much of his philosophy, while at the same time organising his dervish brotherhood around the kitchen. Among the spices that appear in his recipes are cumin, black pepper, cinnamon and sumac.

For Rumi, food was filled with spiritual significance: "I was raw, I was cooked, I was burned." For others it was merely filling. The enjoyment of food was a ceaseless quest, and even in Europe of the Dark Ages, chefs were preparing dishes for pleasure rather than for prolonging their lives. The influence of Islamic Spain and the booty of returning Crusaders revived the gastronomic interest of Roman times. Arab merchants controlled most of this trade, and Arab travellers had some of the most interesting observations to make. During the 14th century, Ibn Battuta spent an unhappy three years in southern India, Ceylon and the Maldives. The cause of his misery was the absence of bread "…eating nothing but rice. I had to help it down with water." The only consolation was the presence of spices in the pickles that accompanied his joyless repasts.

Spices changed every life they touched, and with greater availability after the 17th century, they touched a huge number of lives. As the mystery disappears, scientific discovery proves some of the qualities that were often assumed in the past. The world's rarest produce has now become among the most commonplace. There are a few exceptions, however:

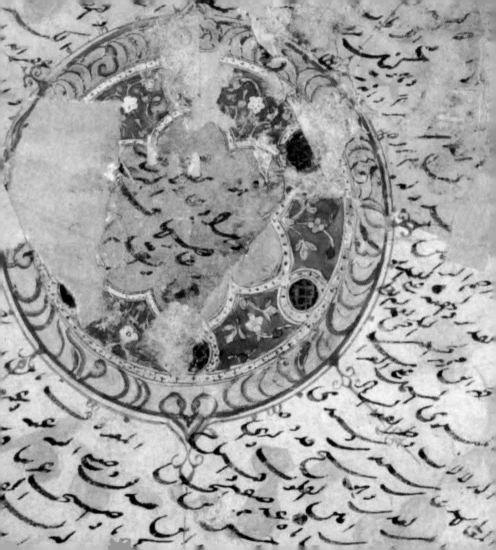

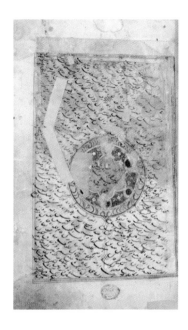

The poetry of the 13th century Sufi master Rumi is filled with references to food

saffron is still worth considerably more than its weight in gold. The most exotic manifestation of spices is now reserved for perfumes. Nina Ricci's classic L'Air du Temps somehow seems more magical when it is revealed that there is bergamot, sandalwood and clove within, as well as the musk that was such a delight to the Seal of the Prophets. How they came to be there is very much a result of the Islamic world's contribution to trade.

Chapter II

> *"While in the souks and in the streets they were burning*
> *incense, sublime camphor, aloe, Indian musk, nadd and*
> *ambergris, and the inhabitants were staining their hands*
> *afresh with henna and their faces with saffron…"*
> *(The Thousand and One Nights)*

How Spices Changed History:
The Incense Road and the spread of Islam

Before the birth of Islam, spices had been vital to southern Arabian commerce. The Romans had called this land *Arabia Felix* ('Fortunate Arabia') because of its prodigious quantities of aromatics. Other parts of the empire were not so blessed; the Latin word for Ireland (*Hibernia*) meant 'wintry'. The south of the Arabian peninsula has been the source of precious natural products for millennia. Among the most highly prized were frankincense and myrrh, used in various cultures for purification and embalming. In the 5th century BC, the Greek historian Herodotus wrote: "Frankincense, myrrh, cassia, cinnamon, and ladanum grow in Arabia alone of all countries... Over the trees that bear frankincense winged snakes stand guard, small in size and varied in appearance, a mass of them about each tree."

Herodotus was wrong about frankincense 'trees' – they are in fact bushes – and the winged snakes that guard them. Despite this, he was right in his assessment of Arabia's importance. Almost four thousand years ago, caravans laboured from the south of the peninsula to the north. Their cargo was deposited in entrepots such as Petra or taken to the Mediterranean coast. The Incense Road was among mankind's earliest known trade routes. In those distant times it received more literary attention than most, appearing in Greek, Roman and Hebrew histories. India was also an essential destination for spice traders. The Romans took a particular interest in the Malabar coast, source of black pepper. They also learned to use the monsoon cycle. This enabled them to sail without the assistance of Arab middlemen who had been the cause of much Roman dissatisfaction.

Since then, one stopping place has grown in significance to become the world's most looked-to city. The Prophet Muhammad ﷺ was part of the Arabian trade route, having married the widow Khadija, a leading Meccan merchant. There are some doubts about exactly what types of goods were traded in Mecca, and the traditional assumption that it was spices has been challenged. One of the most sought-after of all aromatics was known as 'balsam of Mecca', suggesting more than a passing

Mecca was once an important trading centre as well as a place of pilgrimage

acquaintance with that part of the peninsula. Unquestionably, the eventual founder of the Islamic state would have encountered southern Arabian goods on his travels.

Many historians, such as the pivotal Montgomery Watt, see the development of Islam as a direct response to the social conditions *caused* by the spice trade. The inequalities that early Muslims witnessed in Mecca would not have been possible in a nomadic tribal society. It was the breakdown of the earlier society, caused by a mercantile economy, that set Islam on its course. As the new empire grew in the 7th century, it remained inextricably linked to spices. With a spiritual element, commercial success was at last matched by social justice.

Trade opportunities grew as the Arab armies moved out of the peninsula. Their greatest coup came in 641, with the capture of Alexandria, the spice capital of the eastern Mediterranean. New mercantile centres rose and fell. Among the most important of these was Basra, located in what is now southern Iraq. This city expanded from a garrison town to being one of the world's largest metropolises in the 7th and 8th centuries. It was also the birthplace of one of Islam's greatest writers, Al Jahiz. Despite spending decades in Baghdad he clearly lost none of his loyalty to Basra, nor a sense of its essential trading purpose: "Our sea is worth all the others put together, for there is no other into which God has poured so many blessings."

After the conquests of Islam's most expansionary first decades, trade between Europe and the Middle East became as rare as religious dialogue. Christendom sank into the Dark Ages; Islam entered its golden centuries of power and prosperity. From the European point of view, trade with the source of spices dried up, apart from dealings with itinerant Jewish merchants who were considered by Muslims and Christians to be just about acceptable.

At the same time as Europeans were doing their best to keep the Roman spirit of gastronomic diversity from dying completely, Muslim traders were venturing further than ever in search of spices. Tales from the *Thousand and One Nights* show how far they got. Sinbad may have reached Japan. Closer to home, Ali Baba used the name of a spice to open the cave which housed the wealth of the forty thieves.

Arab mariners covered vast distances. This was helped by their knowledge of the monsoon winds, which was far greater than the Romans' had been; the word for monsoon is itself derived from the Arabic word *mawsim*, meaning 'season'. Their most profitable destination was

Ibn Sina's Kitab al-Shifa *is among the most important medical works ever written*

Southeast Asia, source of the most expensive of all spices and eventually to become a significant part of the Islamic world. Arab traders had been visiting the Malay Archipelago long before any part of the region had officially become Muslim. Visitors from other Muslim areas, including India and China, had also prepared the way for widespread conversion. The areas of the Islamic world that accepted the new religion most readily tended to be those which had already experienced the enterprising and equitable approach of Muslim traders. Sub-Saharan Africa, China and Southeast Asia were the main beneficiaries.

Muslims in the Middle Ages were engaged in more than just trading spices. The medical knowledge which came out of this period shows how important the use of these ingredients was. This extended far beyond the borders of Islam. Arabic became the lingua franca of health, and medical treatises were read from northern Europe to Southeast Asia. The image of Islam was never higher than where medicine was involved. The contribution of the 10th century writers Ibn Sina and Al-Zahrawi was vital to universal knowledge. Europe's foremost medieval medical institution also owed a huge debt to Arab scholarship. From the 11th century onwards, the School of Salerno was able to blaze a trail without autos-da-fe, thanks to the input of Islamic-influenced medical specialists such as 'Constantine the African.' Western learning was helped by this as much as Western hygiene was assisted by the Crusaders' encounters.

The gift was more than literary. The practical ability of Muslim physicians was much in demand, and the Persian polymath Al-Razi believed: "All that is written in a book is worth less than the experience of one doctor." Much of that experience entailed knowledge of spices. Ibn Sina, Ibn Rushd and other famous writers were full of praise for everything from cloves to ginger. Later, less well-known authorities were also committed to the power of this medicine. In the 14th century Rashid ud-Din Fadlullah wrote to his son, the governor of Asia Minor, requesting wormwood, anise and agaric for use in his hospital in Tabriz. This facility was equipped with 1,000 Chinese jars, each one labelled with the names of medicinal syrups. Rashid was also well stocked with cloves, cinnamon, nutmeg, cassia, betelnuts and cubebs – a type of pepper that was once regarded very highly and is now making a small comeback.

Military confrontation from the 11th century onwards may not have been the highpoint of Christian-Muslim relations, but the Crusades did at

The closeness between Venice and the Islamic world led to the creation of 'Veneto-Saracenic' wares such as this 15th century copper-alloy bowl

least open eyes on both sides to new trade possibilities. Europe had crawled out of the Dark Ages and was ready to improve its diet once again. The facilitator was Venice. Religious zeal on the Crusaders' part had become such a minor consideration, in 1204 they took the Christian city of Constantinople rather than bothering with Jerusalem. The plan had been devised in Venice and for the next 300 years Venetians dominated trade with the Islamic world.

In addition to Venice, the Renaissance was fuelled by the ports of Genoa, Pisa and Barcelona. Spices were the most popular import in this arrangement, followed by silk. From Europe came the less sensual pleasures of wool and iron. The leading mercantile empires of the Islamic world were the Ottomans and the Mamluks, both of which knew how to harness their economic might. In 1428 the Mamluk Sultan Barsbay is recorded as having imposed a personal monopoly on the pepper trade. As this was Europe's favourite seasoning, consumers were displeased to find the price had doubled. The later Mamluk Sultan Qaitbay was more conciliatory in sending the Doge of Venice precious spices, textiles, porcelain and, for unspecified purposes, a civet horn. A few decades later the Venetians reciprocated with gifts of glass, wool, fur, velvet and Parmesan cheese.

The event that is often thought to have put an end to Venice's supremacy was the discovery of the sea route from Europe to Asia. With the fall of Constantinople to the Ottomans in 1453, Europe needed an alternative to the Asian overland route. Venice was always happy to deal with the highest bidder, but the Ottomans looked set on becoming a serious barrier. In fact, the new rulers of Constantinople turned out to be more commercially minded than expected. They went so far as to model their *sultani* gold coins on the weight and fineness of the most internationally acceptable of all currencies, the Venetian ducat.

Portugal was the pioneer in finding a route that would benefit neither the Venetians nor the Turks. In 1498 Vasco da Gama arrived at the Indian kingdom of Calicut. He returned with the ultimate prize of cloves, ginger, cinnamon and pepper. In the short run this was unfortunate for Venice and for the Muslim rulers who controlled the overland routes. The price of pepper in Venice ended up being several times higher than in Portugal, where huge saving were made on taxes at the cost of innumerable mariners' lives. As the Spanish were also prepared to sacrifice sailors in the cause of cheaper spices, they successfully joined the spice race with Portugal. However, their interests lay more to the West than the East, bringing back previously unknown comestibles such as chocolate and vanilla from the New World, 'discovered' by Christopher Columbus in 1492. The findings of Gavin Menzies in his *1421: The Year China Discovered America* have aroused strong passions for the suggestion that the Americas were first explored by a Chinese Muslim. The 1421 proposal has been abandoned by most scholars, but at least the intrepid Admiral Zheng He is receiving much more attention than he used to for visiting the Malay Peninsula.

The monsoon routes were vital to the spice trade until the arrival of steamships

Even with the overland route being bypassed by the Portuguese, Spanish, Dutch and English, a considerable portion of the spice trade was still in Muslim hands. Many of the destinations from which these cargoes came were Muslim, including the most important components of the Spice Islands: "...the isles of Ternate and Tidore, Whence merchants bring their spicy drugs." These two islands, mentioned in John Milton's *Paradise Lost*, were at one time the only source the world had for clove and nutmeg. Having taken over the area, the Portuguese created a legacy of bad feeling that was continued by the Dutch in their ruthless harvesting of these crops.

Muslim traders were also busy wherever they could avoid the risk of being blasted out of the water by European ships in bitter competition with each other or exercising their monopolies in Southeast Asia. Most of the spice trade was water borne, although the land route continued to exist. After the initial euphoria over Portugal's new sea route, complaints about the quality of their cargoes came in. Venice once again prospered, dealing with whichever Muslim rulers were amenable. In the 15th century there was considerable trade with the Ottomans, including records of the business of Count Giacomo Badoer, who bartered large amounts of Florentine cloth for spices and incense. The Genoese were especially active in importing saffron and sesame from what was then known as 'Turchia'. More surprisingly, the return journey included soap from Europe – a luxury that was not widely associated with Europeans at that time.

The spice route through the Ottoman empire remained intact for many centuries after the Portuguese discoveries in Asia. In the late 18th century Istanbul was still controlling a vast amount of trade. A French observer calculated imports from the East at around five million piastres, of which 'spices and drugs' accounted for 280,000 and pepper 120,000. Business was by no means a one-way street. Among the most unlikely imports into the Ottoman empire was coffee. This had originally been introduced into the West by the Turks, but later shortages had forced them to buy French coffee from the West Indies. Other reversals occurred with products such as indigo, once an Indian monopoly and then exported from America to Asia. Despite these aberrations, there was still approximately 10 times the volume of goods going from East to West than the other way round. Not much has changed over the centuries. According to UN figures, Indonesia is the current major exporter of spices, followed by India, China, Madagascar and Malaysia. The total revenue of these five countries is well over US$1 billion, so it is still a market of some importance. It is also clear that Muslim communities are very much a part of the business.

Chapter III

*"So give what is due to kindred, the needy, and the wayfarer.
That is best for those who seek the Countenance of God, and
it is they who will prosper."*
(Al Quran: Chapter 30, Verse 38)

Rituals of Hospitality: Coffee, Tea, Betel Nut and Incense

In modern times we tend to think of hospitality as that which is shared amongst friends and families. Going back in history the concept was much broader. It meant the welcoming of strangers by offering them not only food, shelter, and protection but also respect, acceptance and friendship. In Islam, rules of courtesy and etiquette (*adab*) have always been paramount. Much emphasis is placed on the proper interrelations between Muslims; individuals are often referred to as brothers or sisters when there may be no blood relationship. The prescribed greeting among Muslims is not an enquiry about health, as it is in many cultures, but is instead *assalamu 'alaikum* (peace be upon you).

The heartland of Islamic belief, Arabia, has a desert climate in which hospitality was held in high esteem and fundamental to spiritual practice. Throughout the peninsula there have long been elaborate ritualised ceremonies. Incense, tea, coffee and, in some areas, betel nut were key to social interaction and maintaining harmony in the community. Disputes were settled, marriages arranged, births celebrated, and contracts sealed with a sip.

The Coffee Ceremony

Coffee, one of the mainstays of modern life around the world, is said to have been discovered in Ethiopia well over a thousand years ago. A colourful anecdote attributing its reviving qualities relates the tale of an Abyssinian goat herder named Khaldi who found his goats frolicking merrily after they ate some wild-growing berries. From Ethiopia, coffee is believed to have travelled via the Red Sea trade routes to Yemen. It is in Yemen that the first commercial cultivation of coffee is thought to have taken place and where many connoisseurs believe the best coffee can still be found.

The English word for coffee is derived from the Turkish *kahveh* which in turn is derived from the Arabic *qahwah*. The most extensive reference to the history, benefits and preparation of coffee is to be found in the 16th century manuscript entitled "Argument in Favour of the Legitimate Use of Coffee". Numerous Muslim scholars have praised the remarkable medicinal and restorative benefits of this stimulant. In the 17th century traders carried this bean to Europe, where great coffee houses developed in Venice, Marseilles, Amsterdam, London and Vienna. As a result of colonial traders the original Arabica beans found their way to Southern India, Indonesia, East Africa, and from Brazil spread to other parts of South and Central America. By the 19th century coffee cultivation was so widespread that Yemen lost its supremacy in the coffee trade.

The bedouin coffee ceremony differs from its urban counterpart in that more emphasis is placed on the action of making coffee than on savouring the results. Guests take great delight in watching the show. Amongst the limited decorative features to be found in a bedouin home, the coffee pot is an ever-present necessity. Coffee is considered to be such an important offering to the guest, that the head of the household undertakes the preparation himself.

A fire is lit and beans are then roasted to the desired colour. They are then placed in a wooden pan to cool. A coffee pot filled with water is placed on the fire while the beans are ground in the meantime. Powdered coffee is added to a second pot with the heated water and put on the fire till it comes to the boil. The gurgling pot signals the host to remove the coffee from the heat. Halfa grass is added to the spout to filter out the grounds. In a third pot, cardamom is added to the old and the

Silver coffee pots were popular among the affluent classes of the Ottoman Empire

new coffee. It is now ready to drink – rich and fragrant. The host then transfers it to another vessel in order to serve it to his guests. As is customary, he takes the first sip to show that the coffee is not tainted in any way. Guests are then offered the coffee in turn, according to their social rank. If the host would like to show his esteem for a particular guest he may do so by offering a cup to him out of turn. The guest is given a cup and sips small amounts, returning it to the host for a refill. Generally, three cups are offered; the last signals that it is time to leave.

The Tea Ceremony of the Maghrib

In the most westerly corner of the Islamic world, the Maghribis favour tea. Tea is akin to the coffee ceremony in this part of North Africa, carrying with it the same overtones of good living and gracious hospitality. In a similar way, water is brought to boil in a kettle. The heated water is added to a distinctively shaped teapot. Usually made of silver, with a bulbous midsection that tapers to the top and finishes in a long spout, this pot is provided with tea, gunpowder (a green tea originating in China) and fresh peppermint leaves. Copious amounts of sugar, broken from a loaf, are added to the pot. The tea is then poured from a height till it froths and is tasted for sweetness and strength. It is then left to steep further before finally being poured into glasses and served on a tray to the awaiting guests. As with coffee, it is customary for a guest to have

*This elaborately
decorated Kashmiri
tea service may have
been used to serve
chai, a favourite
blend of warming
spices*

three glasses. Though consumed throughout the day it is particularly beneficial in aiding digestion at the end of a heavy meal.

The tea offered by Touaregs and other nomadic groups of the Sahara in enamel vessels over makeshift fires is more rustic. However, the concept of hospitality remains just as central to their way of life. In the harsh arid surroundings of the Sahara, where few people have much to offer, it is

the ultimate expression of hospitality. In the desert, the offering of food and drink to a weary traveller is offering the gift of life, and no one is turned away. In these societies, a man is judged by his generosity. On a practical level, hospitality is offered with the understanding that one day the host may become the one in need and a guest himself. Ultimately, the extension of kindness to one's fellow human being is seen as a service to the divine.

Betel Nut

The eating of betel leaves with lime and areca nuts is a widespread practice that ranges from India through Southeast Asia to East Africa and parts of Arabia. In the Malay world, the ceremonial exchange of betel nut and its accompaniments, called *sireh,* forms an intrinsic part of the culture. Its main function is when it is presented in the wedding ceremony as part of a formal exchange of dowry.

The areca nut, which looks like nutmeg, is cut into little pieces and chewed along with betel leaf on which a little lime has been added. It acts as an excellent mouth freshener and digestive aid. Chewing the nut produces a mildly relaxing effect and is said help conversation flow smoothly and without difficulty. Elaborately decorated containers of brass and silver serve to contain the ingredients. The Muslim traveller Ibn Battuta encountered betel nut in Somalia, where it was held in the highest regard. Of its significance and status he says, "The offering of betel is much more important and shows more honour to the recipient than would the gift of silver or gold".

The betel-nut custom is emblematic of Malay culture. This sireh set in silver would have been made for a prosperous patron

*Incense burners with handles
were a convenient way to share
the scent experience with guests*

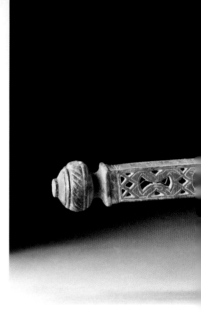

Incense Ceremony

Throughout the Islamic world it is customary to welcome guests with rosewater. The offering of scent is the offering of something precious and engenders a feeling of luxury and well-being. At the conclusion of any meal and after the ritual serving of drinks, incense is burned if one can afford it. In Arabic it is said that incense is 'drunk' (*yashrab bakhur*), as are coffee and tea. Unlike the ritual ceremonies of coffee and tea, in which the male predominates, women here are the masters of preparation. After being prepared, the incense is passed on to the head of the household to offer and honour their guests.

Plumes of perfumed smoke, heavy with the scent of caravans of frankincense, myrrh and oudh, steeped in tradition and history rise from the glowing embers of the brazier. These receptacles can be made simply of clay or brass while the more elaborate versions are crafted with silver and gold. The vessel is passed around and men perfume their beards, hair and clothes; a scent which lingers on them long after they have left the gathering. According to the rules of politesse, the incense signals that it is time to head home. A traditional Arab saying says "praise yourself with incense and go" (*bakhir wa ruh*).

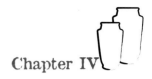

Chapter IV

*"There is no disease that Allah has created,
except that He has also created its treatment."*
(Hadith, Al-Bukhari)

Practical Application: Scents, Cosmetics and Medicine

The Islamic world maintained the use of scents in the form of resins such
as myrrh and frankincense that were burned to purify the environment
and to perfume clothes. These substances had long been prized in
Mediterranean lands; at the dawn of the first century AD, they were seen
as a fitting tribute at the nativity of Jesus. The word perfume itself comes
from the Latin *'perfumum'* ('by smoke') referring to fragrant substances
which were offered to the gods. This idea of the sacred quality of scent
pervaded the understanding of traditional man. The earliest known
perfumes are attributed to the Egyptians, who developed a technique for
capturing the scent of flowers called *enfleurage* that is still widely used
today. In this method petals are placed with pure animal fat until the
scent is absorbed by the fat. These pomades are then applied as scented
ointments to the skin. This is still the best and costliest method for
extracting a quality substance available to perfumers today. Another
method involved the use of hot oil for extraction.

Perfume containers (attardan) such as these were often made from precious materials, reflecting the considerable value of their contents

Later, this love for scent would be coupled with scientific techniques in the work of the famous alchemist al-Kindi, forming the basis for a perfumery industry. The *Book of Perfume, Chemistry and Distillation*, written in the 9th century, is the earliest extant treatise of its kind and describes in detail the process for distilling rose water. Since then the extraction process has remained much the same in the Islamic world. Aromatic flowers and spices are placed into a sealed copper vessel which contains water and rests on a wood or dung fire. The arising vapours then pass through a cooling tube to collect in another smaller copper vat, which rests below the larger one. The cooled distillate is then blended with a carrier oil, such as sandalwood, which acts as a natural preservative preventing the corruption of the scent. The term 'attar' has now come to refer to any distillate of flowers, roots, spices and herbs or blend thereof.

These Oriental attars are unisex in nature, rather than the gender-specific fragrances of the West. Unlike conventional modern perfumes, which use an alcohol base to increase the quantity and preserve the quality of the perfume, attars are still being produced in the Islamic world without alcohol – an element that is far from being considered halal. The scent of these attars is generally much stronger than their Western counterparts as no dilution occurs. Instead, there is an intensification of the qualities of the flower so that in smelling a drop of rose oil, for example, a whole field can be imagined. Natural perfumes have the added benefit of evolving with one's own body chemistry. That is why the same scent on two people can smell so very different. Commercial perfumes, often made with synthetic substances, tend to be rather one dimensional in nature. Attars have the added benefit of being readily absorbed into the skin and carry with them the therapeutic value of essential oils. The attars that were brought back by Crusaders contributed to the development of the perfume industry and its technology in Europe, especially in centres such as Grasse in France.

Attars of this sort can still be found in the traditional bazaars (*souq*) of the Islamic world. A more commercial composition such as Amouage (the name suggesting 'waves' of sensory pleasure induced by perfume) is an undertaking by the Sultan of Oman to revive the traditions of Arabian perfumery. The sumptuous and costly ingredients are based on traditional ingredients found in the Arab world. The legendary silver frankincense of the incense route takes centre stage in its formulation. Amouage serves as an interesting case study for a commercially viable product based on traditional Islamic culture.

Elaborately decorated containers were used to hold powdered antimony (kohl) - used to prevent eye infections and believed to ward off the evil eye

Containers such as this apothecary's box served as portable dispensaries for travelling physicians in an age before the invention of packaged medicines

In the arid climate of the Middle East, it is not difficult to imagine that the need for protective ointments arose. Eye makeup such as mascara, lipstick and powder all have their earliest recorded sources amongst the Egyptians, Mesopotamians and Sumerians. Kohl, powdered antimony, is used to this day by Arab women as a protection against eye diseases and as an ornament. In the traditional baths or *hammam*, women ritualised the bathing process by beautifying themselves with oils, dying their hair and bodies with henna, and perfuming themselves with attars.

Unani: Graeco-Arab Scent Therapy

In order to develop an understanding of the role that scents and cosmetics played in traditional Islamic societies, it is important to understand the activity and purpose for buying scent. In medieval societies it was often the herbalist or apothecary who blended perfumes. These perfumes – much in keeping with the traditional aromatherapy used today – were valued not only for the olfactory pleasure they could give but also for their medicinal benefits. In Arabic the word for floral essence is *itr*, from which the word attar is derived. Any oil of a plant contains its life force and essential nature.

A more encompassing understanding forms the basis for healing practices in Islam. *Tibb*, an Arabic word, comprises all medicine of the physical, mental or spiritual realms. In fact, physicians (*hakim*) were often skilled spiritual practitioners and members of many Sufi circles were renowned for their healing knowledge.

Unani medicine was first introduced and developed by the Greek physician Hippocrates (460-377 BC) and Galen (131-210 AD). This was later developed into a full-fledged therapeutic system by Ibn Sina, known as Avicenna in the West and known in the East as 'the Prince of Physicians'. His *Kitab al-Shifa'* (The Book of Healing) developed his theories of medicine and its allied sciences. His second book, *Al-Qanun fi'l at-Tibb* (The Canon of Medicine) describes over 760 medicinal plants and drugs. Arab pharamacists were the first to introduce new drugs such as camphor, sandalwood, musk, myrrh, cassia, tamarind, nutmeg, cloves, aconite, ambergris and mercury. Medicinal drinks (*sharbats*) were also developed, often flavoured with rose or orange flower water as a way of making medicines more palatable.

Unani relies on the diagnosis of the pulse and is dependent on the four humours. This principle was based on the belief that the body was composed of the same four elements as found in the world (earth, air, fire, and water), each found in people to a lesser or greater degree. When these humours were out of balance, sickness occurred. The use of fragrance to alter the physiology of mind and body is a subtle discipline within the larger scope of Unani medicine. Attars were utilised alone or blended as the Hakim (physician) directed. For example, violet was reputed to be a favourite of the Prophet Muhammad ﷺ, and rose is said to be an excellent restorative and antidepressant.

'Albarello' jars acquired a huge pharmaceutical importance, being used almost exclusively for housing medicines

Definitive Dishes
of the Islamic World

Spices are the essence of food in many cultures, especially those of the Islamic world. From the Malay Archipelago to the Maghrib the range of ingredients is immense, but the approach is often similar: bringing life to a dish with a select combination of flavourings.

Starting in the east of the Islamic world are the full-flavoured offerings of Malay cuisine. This region has always been the source of the most sought-after spices, including cloves and nutmeg. Among the quintessential Malay offerings is *pajeri*. This dish is exceptional for the wide variety of dried spices that it incorporates. Combining sweetness and sourness in a thick creamy sauce, the main ingredient is usually aubergine or pineapple – in which case it can look misleadingly like potato. As with much of the pride of Malay cuisine, it is seen most frequently at celebrations. Few feasts take place without *pajeri* and *rendang*.

Pineapple Pajeri

Ingredients

1 pineapple (sliced)
5 tablespoons palm oil
2 cms ginger
5 shallots
5 cloves of garlic
3 tablespoons coriander powder
1 tablespoon fennel powder
1 tablespoon cumin powder
2 tablespoons chilli powder
1 tablespoon turmeric

2 sticks cinnamon
5 cloves
5 cardamom seeds
5 star anise
3 tablespoons *kerisik*
(roasted grated coconut)
mixed with a little water
Water
Salt and sugar to taste
4 de-seeded green chillies

Preparation

Cut pineapple into circles or quarters and boil in hot water until slightly cooked and tender. In a separate frying pan, heat palm oil. Add in the sliced ginger, shallots and garlic. Add all the spices, *kerisik* and some water. Simmer until the oil appears to have separated from the gravy. Lastly, add in the cooked pineapple and sliced green chillies. Season with sugar and salt. Serve with rice.

Dal

This lentil dish is comfort food found throughout the Indian Subcontinent and in Indian restaurants around the world. Usually served with rice or a variety of different breads, it can also be savoured as a soup. The type of lentil used determines the character of the dish.

Garam masala, used in *dal*, is a ubiquitous component of the Subcontinental culinary tradition. Although the name of this medley of dry roasted spices literally means "hot spice blend", it is a pungent rather than a chilli heat that it gives off. While off-the-shelf blends can be purchased for the sake of time and convenience, serious cooks prefer to create their own; commercially prepared blends are liable to lose their freshness. It is used as a seasoning for finished dishes, providing a highly aromatic addition to many dishes and is an aid to digestion.

Typical proportions of *garam masala* are as follows, lightly roasted in a shallow pan and then ground in a spice grinder:
20 grams black pepper
10 grams cloves
20 grams cinnamon
15 grams cardamom
10 grams cumin seed
10 grams bay leaves
5 grams coriander seed

Dal

Ingredients

1 cup dal (moong dal,
toor dal,or yellow split peas)
4 to 5 cups water
1 tablespoon minced ginger
6 to 8 cloves minced garlic
1 medium chopped onion
2 medium chopped tomatoes

2 teaspoons turmeric
2 tablespoon oil or ghee
2 teaspoons garam masala
Coriander or parsley as
garnish
Salt to taste

Preparation

Wash the dal repeatedly until the water clears, then drain. Boil with fresh water
in a heavy saucepan, cover and simmer. Lower heat, add turmeric and salt.
Simmer gently for about 1 1/2 hours, stirring occasionally until the dal is soft.
Add more water if the soup becomes too thick. Whisk until consistency is
smooth. In a separate pan, lightly fry garlic, ginger, onion and tomatoes in two
tablespoons of oil or ghee. Add to dal mixture. Simmer for another 15 minutes.
Garnish with coriander and garam masala and serve with fragrant basmati rice.

Baharat

Cuisine in the Levant makes plentiful use of the spice blend known as *baharat*. The name is derived from the word for pepper "bahar" and refers to a spice blend with a strong component of black pepper. Other standard ingredients are allspice, nutmeg, cloves, cardamom and cinnamon. In a dish such as prawn balls, the sweetness of fresh seafood is balanced by the piquancy of the *baharat*.

These are the classic proportions of key *baharat* ingredients:
250 grams black pepper
250 grams allspice
100 grams cinnamon
100 grams cloves
100 grams cardamom
200 grams dried rose buds
6 pieces nutmeg

Prawn Balls

Ingredients

1 kilo uncooked peeled prawns
1/4 cup fresh coriander
3/4 teaspoon turmeric
1 teaspoon salt
3/4 cup ground rice
3 tablespoons ghee or butter
1 cup finely chopped onion
2 teaspoons baharat mix

2 tablespoons lemon zest
1 piece tamarind (5 cms)
2 cups water
1 small onion
1 large tomato, peeled and chopped
1/4 teaspoon hot chilli pepper
2 teaspoons sugar

Preparation

Blend prawns with coriander leaves into a paste. Add turmeric, ground rice and salt. Mix well, cover and refrigerate. Lightly fry one cup of onions in two tablespoons of ghee until transparent. Stir in one teaspoon of baharat plus lemon peel. Set aside. Push pre-soaked tamarind through sieve. Saute the remaining onion with one tablespoon ghee until transparent. Add the tamarind liquid, one cup of warm water, one teaspoon baharat, tomato, chilli pepper and sugar. Cover and simmer for 15 minutes. Take one tablespoon of prawn paste and flatten. Place one teaspoon of reserved onion mixture in the centre and push prawn paste around this to form a ball. Add the prawn balls to the simmering sauce. Cover and simmer over for around 30 minutes.

Saffron

Saffron, hand-picked crocus stamens, is perhaps the world's costliest spice. Its fiery colour and spectacular aroma are unmistakable. Opinions differ on which saffron is the best, with many putting Kashmir or Iran in that category. As production is very limited in those locations, Spanish saffron is more widely used.

In this recipe for Milanese risotto, the historic trade routes of East and West come to life, creating a true fusion cuisine. The brilliant colour of saffron is the perfect complement to the buttery and rich grains of creamy rice.

Milanese Risotto

Ingredients
7 cups chicken or vegetable stock
2 cups arborio rice
1/2 medium Spanish onion, finely chopped
3 cloves garlic, finely chopped
3 tablespoons olive oil
2 tablespoons coarsely chopped fresh tarragon
1 tablespoon saffron
1 tablespoon honey
Salt and freshly ground pepper

Preparation
Simmer stock in a saucepan. Heat the olive oil over medium heat and heat the onion and garlic until soft. Add the rice and saffron, stirring until the rice is coated with oil. Cook for two minutes. Add 1 cup of stock. Stir until absorbed. Repeat with a second cup. Add stock in 1/2 cup increments, cooking and stirring until it is absorbed. Keep adding stock until all is absorbed. Complete with honey and tarragon; season to taste.

Cinnamon

The name of the spice evokes Sri Lanka, although it has been used all over the world. In the time-honoured process, the bark of the cinnamon tree is cut from the trunk and left to dry. The result is a versatile spice filled with both sweet and spicy flavours. It is a popular element in desserts, even appearing in some of England's blander puddings. Within the Islamic world, it is an enduringly essential part of Moroccan *bastilla*, in which its sweet spicy flavours are brought out to great effect.

Moroccan Bastilla

Ingredients

1/2 chicken
1 chopped onion
1 whole cinnamon stick
1/2 teaspoon turmeric
1/2 teaspoon ginger
teaspoon black pepper
1 cup chopped coriander

6 eggs
200 grams almonds
1/2 cup sugar
2 tablespoons cinnamon
2 large sheets phyllo pastry dough 1/2
1/4 cup melted butter

Preparation

Boil chicken with onion and spices for about 30 minutes. Drain and reserve approximately 1/4 cup of liquid. Bone the chicken and cut the meat. Cook the six eggs with reserved cooking liquid until soft scrambled. Mix the eggs with the chicken meat. Coarsely blend almonds with sugar and cinnamon in a food processor. Unfold a layer of phyllo pastry slightly more than halfway across the butter-smeared pan. Repeat over the other half of the pan so that pastry overlaps. Spread 1/3 cup of the almond mixture on the dough. This is followed by the chicken and egg mixture and then another layer of almonds. Fold the phyllo and brush top with melted butter. Bake for 12 to 15 minutes in a $180^{\circ c}$ oven, until lightly browned. Invert pan on a plate to remove the bastilla and garnish with powdered cinnamon and sugar.

Flower Waters (Rose and Orange Blossom)

Popular throughout the Islamic world, from the Maghrib to India, these waters are used to add flavour to teas, sweets and cordials. Rose and orange blossom waters are valued for their medicinal properties in cooling the body and aiding digestion. Their most obvious quality is the powerful floral aroma they exude.

Muhallebili is a light and creamy milk-pudding recipe that is subtly scented with the presence of roses. Originally from the Ottoman world, this dish highlights the exceptional aromatic quality of rose water, although orange-blossom works well as a substitute.

Rose-water Milk Pudding

Ingredients

3 tablespoons cornflour

3 cups milk

2 tablespoons sugar

5 tablespoons icing sugar

4 tablespoons rosewater

Preparation

Mix the cornflour and sugar with the milk. Stir until thickened over medium heat and then cook for an additional four to five minutes. Pour the mixture to a depth of around two centimetres in a shallow bowl. Chill when cool. For presentation, cut into squares or place on individual plates. Sprinkle liberally with rosewater and icing sugar.

Cardamom

Cardamom is hand picked and expensive. The green pod is filled with a flavour and aroma reminiscent of bergamot, camphor and lemon. Originally cultivated in Kerala on the Malabar coast, its popularity spread far from there. During the Middle Ages, Christian crusaders returning from Palestine brought cardamom to many parts of northern Europe, where it is still widely used for baking. It provides an unexpected layer of taste to bread and cakes.

Cardamom is also used prodigiously in coffee. According to the importance of the occasion, or the guest, larger quantities are added. This spice provides a greenish tint and a grassy aroma in perfect balance with the coffee. For the flavour of the spice to be really apparent, it cannot be stinted on.

Arabian Coffee

Ingredients
4 cups of water
4 heaped teaspoons Arabian coffee
A large pinch of ground cardamom

Preparation
Measure the water and place in a coffee pot, preferably the long-handled type
from the Middle East. Add the coffee and cardamom, without stirring. Place on
high heat for three minutes and stir halfway through this. As the coffee begins to
rise, remove from the heat before it boils. As the froth lowers, bring back to the
heat and remove as soon as it starts to boil. Serve immediately.

Ras-al-hanout

This blend of aromatic herbs and spices originated in Morocco and is used throughout North Africa. As expected with a name that means "top of the shop", it is a medley of the most superior spices. There are many different versions of *ras-al-hanout*. Ranging from a dozen spices to well over a hundred, the most likely ingredients include cardamom, mace, nutmeg, cinnamon and chilli. For a more unusual approach, there are grains of paradise and dried rosebuds. As an ideal end to a meal with the fragrance and delicacy of *ras-al-hanout*, sip mint tea to aid digestion.

Couscous With Roasted Vegetables And Feta

Ingredients

5 garlic cloves
3 tablespoons virgin olive oil
5 bell peppers
Salt and pepper
4 quartered ripe tomatoes
1 large red onion, sliced
300 grams cubed sheep milk feta

vegetable stock: 1 1/2 times the volume of couscous
300 grams couscous
4 teaspoons ras-al-hanout
2 tablespoons butter
1/4 cup fresh pine nuts
1/4 cup chopped parsley
200 grams pitted olives

Preparation

Mix crushed garlic with olive oil, salt and pepper. Toss with the tomatoes, peppers and onion. Remove the vegetables and roast in a preheated oven (200°) for around 30 to 40 minutes. Add feta and olives to the pan after the vegetables are removed, and then add to the vegetables. Make couscous using vegetable stock or water and add ras-al-hanout and butter. Mix vegetables and couscous together and serve hot, topped with parsley and lightly toasted pine nuts.

Appendix

Spices commonly found in blends. All these spices are common components of spice blends whether in Indian *masalas*, Arab *baharat*, or North African *ras-al-hanout*.

Pepper
Growing abundantly on the western coast of India, pepper is literally the spice of life. Its excellent digestive qualities make it ideal for use in spice blends. Pepper comes in a variey of colours, from the common black and white to green and pink.

Nutmeg and Mace
Nutmeg is a bitter lemony spice, generally used in small quantities. Mace, the outer red web-like covering, is dried and has a sharper flavour. It grows traditionally in Granada, Indonesia, India and Sri Lanka.

Clove
The sweet spicy scent of cloves, resembling pepper and carnations, is synonymous with Indonesia. Arab traders in the region were responsible for distributing it. Today, however, most of the Indonesian crop is used locally. Zanzibar is the main exporter of the spice. While cloves do not figure principally in any dishes, they complement meat stews and are often used to flavour rice.

Cumin

Egypt is undoubtedly the land of *kamun* (cumin), as a trip to the Khan al-Khalili will confirm. This spice is found in the cuisines of the Mediterranean, from Spain and Morocco to Egypt and the Levant, as well as in Iran and India. It is a popular ingredient in a variety of spice blends.

Sumac

This spice comes from the berries of a wild bush that grows in Mediterranean areas. It is widely used in Arabic cooking, where it lends a sour note akin to lemons. The berries are usually dried and ground into a coarse red powder that is sprinkled on food. *Zatar*, a blend of sumac and thyme, is a popular spice blend used to flavour labni, a cream cheese made from yogurt.

List of Illustrations